D1614308

THE
SEXUALLY
DELICIOUS
MARRIAGE

BOOKS BY NAURA HAYDEN

The Sexually Delicious Marriage

How To Satisfy A Woman <u>Every</u> <u>Time</u> . . .
and have her beg for more!

How To Satisfy A <u>Man</u> Every Time . . .
and have him beg for more!

GO$\overset{O}{\wedge}$D Is Alive and Well and Living
in Each One of Us

Everything You've Always Wanted To Know
About ENERGY . . . but were too weak to ask

Isle Of View (Say It Out Loud)!

Astro-Logical Love

The Hip, High-Prote, Low-Cal, Easy-Does-It
Cookbook

THE
SEXUALLY
DELICIOUS
MARRIAGE

. . . intimate answers for a
long, exciting, faithful, marriage

by
NAURA HAYDEN

Bibli O'Phile Books, Inc.
New York, New York

Distributed by Penguin Group USA

Thank you, Rick Kramer

Copyright © 2008 by Naura Hayden

Published by Bibli O'Phile Books
NHU Enterprises, 1504 N US Highway 395
Gardnerville, NV 89410

Printed in Canada

Library of Congress Catalog Card Number 2008903422

ISBN-13: 978-0-942104-19-6

Distributed by Penguin Group USA

10 9 8 7 6 5 4 3 2 1

To Good, which is God....
which is Good....
which is God....
which is Love....
which is God....
which is Love....
which is God....
which is Love

God, with infinite wisdom, gave us the enchantment of sex so that together we may joyfully pleasure each other and create a loving bond that will last a lifetime.

Contents

Author's Note

You cannot have the quadruple whammy of physical, mental, emotional, and spiritual ecstasy unless sex is between two people who love each other.

I believe that sex and love belong together in a loving, faithful, committed, married relationship.

This is a marriage manual.

Foreword

Love is caring for one or many persons.

"In love" is love with sexual desire for one person only.

As long as two people stay sexually "in love", they will never part.

Because I believe that marriage is the greatest relationship two people can have, and sexual pleasure is the greatest gift two people can give to each other, that gift of pleasure belongs in the loving relationship of marriage.

Two people first become friends, then best friends who love each other, and then when that love grows and they fall "in love" (because their sexual desire for each other is overwhelming), they decide they want to become partners for life and get married.

They will overcome all problems—money troubles, business failures, armed forces or other separations, problem kids, sickness—there is _nothing_ that can hurt their marriage as long as they stay sexually in love.

Now again, the most important part of any relationship is love, and certainly it's the most important part of marriage. But the very deepest expression of that love is sex.

You can hold hands, hug or kiss, but you cannot get any closer mentally, emotionally, spiritually and of course physically than in a sexual union. When you're in love and you make love, you surrender sexually to each other and become spiritually one.

When you realize the difference between "love" and "in love" you'll realize how very important exciting delicious sex is that keeps you "in love."

Marriage without exciting sex is between two roommates.

Marriage with exciting sex is between a husband and wife who will do anything to keep their marriage sexually exciting and faithful.

As long as two people stay sexually "in love", they will never part.

Introduction

I wrote my first marriage manual, *How to Satisfy a Woman Every Time ... and have her beg for more!* (which came out in 1981 and is still going strong), because I had never had an orgasm through intercourse alone.

Other ways, yes, but never intercourse.

Then I came up with a new technique that enables a husband to make his wife have an orgasm using only intercourse every single time they make love. This was after years of sexual frustration on my part. I was so overjoyed that I didn't have to wonder what was wrong with me anymore, and I also didn't have to fake it anymore.

And many millions of women responded just as I did. I received thousands of letters from husbands and wives, particularly wives telling me how they look forward to making love with their husbands who now know how to make them "come" every time, but also husbands saying they don't have to beg their wives to make love anymore.

There are hundreds of books out about other forms of lovemaking—oral sex, sex toys, hand sex, different positions, sadistic/masochistic sex, gay sex, etc.—but my first marriage manual is only about intercourse, which, if done correctly, is the greatest sexual pleasure a man can give his wife, an orgasm using only his penis.

It's almost impossible for a woman to have an orgasm during intercourse alone (no fingers, no hands, no tongue, just penis), without that technique, and that's why the book became a runaway bestseller.

It was twice on *The New York Times* bestseller hardcover list ten years apart—first for ten weeks, second for sixty-two weeks, #1.

Amazingly, it sold well for those ten years in between and never stopped. It's printed in twenty-two languages, in twenty-seven foreign countries, plus in Braille for the blind.

Publishers Weekly reported it was the #1 bestselling hardcover book in the U.S. in 1992. Up till now it's sold almost three million hardcover books and is still selling in bookstores and on the web because of word-of-mouth—wives telling their girlfriends and husbands telling their buddies.

In this newest marriage manual, *The Sexually Delicious Marriage*, I've come up with the ultimate sexual foreplay targeting not a woman's clitoris, but a different part of her body, arousing her more than she's ever been aroused before.

It's the most powerful female sexual stimulation that exists, and when her husband uses it, he will turn her on, making her so hot that she'll begin her sexual surrender that will only be complete when she later has an orgasm.

And a woman cannot fake this foreplay. Her husband will find that now he's in charge of her body—and he's really making her hot.

That's the giant turn-on for both of them—once he starts the foreplay, he starts to take charge of her body, and she starts to sexually surrender to him.

An orgasm is sexual surrender for both the wife and the husband.

This is the reason an "in love" orgasm is so overwhelming—a woman knowing that her husband has the power to give her this incredible pleasure, and a man knowing that his wife has the same power over him.

Certainly anyone can have an orgasm without love, but every person reading this knows how empty and meaningless that can be. Sure, it's a temporary great physical feeling, but not what we're each looking for.

That's the reason each one of us is searching for that one special person with whom we can fall in love and live with "till death do us part." And have exciting sex with as often as possible.

Again, an orgasm is sexual surrender, but not surrender in any way but sexually to his or her mate.

They are both still in charge of their money, their friends, their everything-they-want-to-be-in-charge-of, but sexually they have to surrender to each other, holding nothing back, giving themselves totally to each other. They have to let down all the mental and emotional barriers in order for them to fall more deeply in love and have the most intense and pleasure-full orgasms they've ever had. And those orgasms get better with time.

When her husband begins this special foreplay, his wife will begin her surrender to him. It won't be a total surrender because that only happens with orgasm, but it will be so powerful that she will get very close to orgasm, more than she's ever gotten before with foreplay.

For many women this ultimate foreplay will be the beginning of falling back in love with their husbands. And the beginning of many men falling back in love with their wives.

This "teasing" foreplay makes her body so hot and receptive to her husband that she'll want to keep making love till she climaxes. It could be either that day or night, or the next day, or even a week later.

Her body will respond completely to this gentle stimulation and will keep her in a constant state of arousal till her husband does it again and/or makes her have an orgasm.

And then when he again caresses her body, her desire for him will start all over again, a never-ending sexually delicious excitement.

A form of this foreplay is something that's been done throughout history many billions of trillions of times by husbands to their wives, but it's always been a secondary event, a perfunctory thirty to sixty second addendum preceding the "main event", intercourse. It's never been a preliminary event by itself.

Until now.

If he teases her body with this sexual foreplay for ten minutes in the morning and then either one of them or both have to leave for work, she will think of little else except when he's going to drive her wild again.

And the powerful side effect of the teasing of her body that he's doing to make her sexually crazed is that seeing and knowing that what he's doing to her is driving her wild with passion also greatly arouses him.

It turns him on to see his wife get so hot and excited, and when he starts to feel he can't continue without getting on top and making love to her, he'll have to use strong discipline to make sure his own orgasm won't begin.

Then when he finally feels it's time to stop teasing her body, he will make both of them surrender to each other in explosive orgasms of love.

It's so powerful that once he overwhelms her body with arousal, she'll be counting the hours or days till he'll do it again.

I've been aware for many years of how doing this for thirty seconds or ninety seconds is stimulating as a prelude to other sex.

But I wasn't aware at all then as I am now of how powerful this sexual foreplay is when done, not as a prelude, but as a sexual excitement in and of itself.

Before I wrote *How To Satisfy A Woman* I had never experienced this sexual power over my body, but I have now. It's the most intense, exciting sexual feeling I've ever had for an extended period of time.

An orgasm can last only a few moments, but this teasing foreplay can go on for many minutes, even an hour. And it will drive her wild and make her fall in love even deeper with the man who's sexually teasing her, the man she married.

As long as two people stay sexually "in love", they will never part.

1
Delicious Sex
Can Overcome
Anything

The #1 cause of divorce has always been reported in court statistics to be financial problems.

But as I've discussed on numerous TV and radio shows, if the sex is really great and exciting for both partners, not just the husband but also the wife, they could have overwhelming financial problems and not let the problems do them in.

Eviction notices, salary garnishes, judgments, etc. could be hounding them, but with love and exciting delicious sex, they'll work as a team to figure out how to solve the money problems so they can continue living and loving together and having more exciting sex.

Until you have experienced incredibly delicious sex with the man or woman you're in love with, you'll never know what you've missed.

Until your body is trembling inside with excitement of the anticipation of your mate making you explode with passion, you haven't entered "heaven-on-earth":

the emotionally peaceful place of being with the man or woman you truly love,

the mentally peaceful place of knowing that nothing on earth is as important as being with the mate you truly love,

the physically peaceful place of having your body totally relaxed and filled with the joy of true love, the spiritually peaceful place of knowing that God/Good guided you to your mate for you to know love and goodness and peace that will be with you forever.

According to most statistics, sex is #5 in the list of causes for divorce. But I've always believed, and believe even more now, that sex is and always has been the first and most important cause for divorce.

If your mate doesn't want to, or isn't willing to, do everything in his or her power to make you happy sexually—or if you don't want to, or aren't willing to, do everything in your power to make your mate happy sexually, then you know you're not really "in love".

You most probably love each other, but without being "in love", it's not enough to withstand the problems that often happen in a marriage.

Maybe she doesn't want to make love and he does, or he doesn't want to and she does. And they sure don't turn each other on anymore. They don't hold hands, they don't caress each other—they give quick pecks on the cheek, not passionate kisses on the lips.

Whatever reason, it leads to divorce, and is usually masquerading as financial problems, children problems, etc. because people don't usually want to open up to a judge about their sexual problems. And probably most times they're not even aware that the real reason is sex.

I don't believe most women understand how important *exciting* sex is to marriage. I think most men do, but they don't know how to *keep* it exciting.

Of course we've all been taught about the importance of love, but there are many forms of love.

Many years ago I did in-depth research to find out exactly what love is. And unknown to me, my late friend Warren Avis (Avis Rent-a-Car) was researching the very same thing. He also wanted to find out exactly what love is all about. And once I found out we were both on the same track, we met and compared our notes. We were anxious to find out the details of what the other had researched and discovered.

What both of us found, after many months of research and interviews with husbands, wives, mothers and fathers, is that the bottom-line meaning of love is caring.

You love your plants, you take care to water them and make sure they have some sunlight in order to thrive.

You love your dog and pussycat and care for both of them, so you feed them both, and walk your dog often, and you make sure your pussycat's litter box is clean, so they both can thrive.

You love your kids and care for them by feeding them healthy nourishing food, giving them warm clothes, making sure they do their homework and then getting enough sleep, driving them to music lessons or baseball practice, and giving them everything they need to thrive.

You love your spouse and take care that he or she eats well, sleeps well, and knows how much you love him or her so your marriage can thrive.

But in order for him or her to really know and feel how much you care and how important it is to you to keep the love in your marriage strong, you have to do something much more important than cook gourmet meals, mow the lawn, take the clothes to the dry cleaners, fix the loose floorboard in the hall, or be a loving mom or dad to your kids.

You have to understand the great importance of not just sex, but exciting, delicious sex.

Many years ago in the 1930s and 40s, Ingrid Bergman was a very beautiful and famous movie star in Hollywood who was married to a Swedish neurosurgeon, Dr. Petter Lindstrom. Their young daughter, Pia Lindstrom, later became a well-known TV news correspondent in New York City, and won several awards including two Emmys for her work.

In the late 1940s Ingrid Bergman became a big fan of an Italian film director, Roberto Rossellini, who had just made two small budget films, *Open City* and *Paisan* in 1946 and '47. He and his two films got enormous attention for their "neorealism", and Ingrid wrote him a letter telling him how much she admired him and his films. She offered to work with him, they met several times, and she loved his Italian temperament. In 1949 they arranged for her to star in a small film that he was soon to make, *Stromboli Terra Di Dio*, to be filmed on the island of Stromboli off the north coast of Sicily.

Up to that point Ingrid had starred in several great movies, *Intermezzo*, *Saratoga Trunk*, *Spellbound* and *Notorious*, and had been nominated for an Academy Award for other leading roles in great movies: *For Whom The Bell Tolls*, *Joan of Arc*, and *The Bells of St. Mary's*. She finally won the coveted Academy Award for her role in *Gaslight*, (she later won two more Academy Awards for *Anastasia* and *Murder On The Orient Express*).

The movie she's most famous for is *Casablanca* (my all-time favorite flick) in her role as "Ilsa", co-starring Humphrey Bogart as "Rick", a story about the tragic happenings of World War II.

So you can see what a gigantic movie star she was, starring in Academy Award winning movies, and how unusual it was for her to want to star in a small budget film in Italy. She was obviously smitten with him.

She left for Stromboli in 1949 and her whole life changed. She fell totally, passionately in love with Rossellini, stayed with him in Italy and left her husband and daughter behind in Hollywood.

Ingrid and Roberto had three children, one son, Robertino, born out-of-wedlock, and after she was finally granted a divorce from her husband, she married Rossellini in 1950 and had twin daughters, Ingrid and Isabella. Because of her illicit romance and out-of-wedlock son, she was blackballed not only in Hollywood but in the whole U.S.A.

Ingrid Bergman gave up everything she loved that was important to her—her husband, her daughter, and her career as one of the greatest movie stars of all-time—to stay with the man she fell in love with.

Her story highlights the difference between love and in-love, and shows us how powerful and *overwhelming* "in love" sexual attraction for just one person is. It's led to the breakup of millions of families, the breaking of millions of hearts.

Unfortunately for Ingrid, Roberto was compulsively unfaithful and jealous of her working for other film directors, and their marriage in 1950 ended seven years later.

We've read or heard of hundreds, even thousands of men and women who lost everything because of their overwhelming sexual need to fall "in love". We've seen that the need for sexual excitement is enough for many people to risk losing *everything* important in their lives.

When you fall "in-love" with someone, and both of you *stay* in-love, that in-love sexual attraction will never leave.

Whenever sex is not exciting and delicious, it becomes boring for either partner or both.

It's not enough for the wife to just lie there and have her husband "put it in" and pump away till he has his orgasm.

You don't have to think much about it to see how boring that would become after a short period of time.

It's also not enough for the husband to insert his erect penis into his wife's vagina and think it must feel as good to her as it does to him. If it did, believe me she wouldn't just lie there inert while he does his pumping.

If he knew how to intercourse the right way to make it feel good, she'd be doing things other than just passively lying there.

Once a husband learns how to do the "ultimate foreplay", his wife will be so hot she'll never "fake it" again. All a woman wants is for her husband to know how to turn her on and then do it.

Her body aches for him to make her hot and give her the same ecstasy as he gets every time they make love.

And of course, if wives knew what to tell their husbands to do to turn them on, they would. Women were and are just as ignorant as men in this area. And I was as clueless as everyone else.

I knew nothing about exciting foreplay or "missionary position" pleasure until after years of faking I finally figured out what my husband could do to make me have an orgasm with just his penis in intercourse, and I wrote *HTSAWoman*.

But I still hadn't figured out incredibly exciting foreplay. That came later.

Believe me, I thought and felt every one of those frustrated sexual feelings that all women have felt at one time or another, the "getting to the edge of the cliff and never going over", and I was very unhappy.

Just for your info, there's no such thing as a "frigid" woman, there are only husbands who don't know how to make their wives "hot".

And wives who are just as much in the dark.

Once a man learns how to drive his wife wild with desire for an orgasm, and then be able to give her one through intercourse alone, it's a turning point in that marriage.

When his wife knows that every time they start making love her husband will do things to her body he's never done before—the "ultimate foreplay" that will drive her crazy with desire—and will lead to an orgasm for her, she'll want to make love often.

There won't be any more "headaches". She will now get to the edge of the cliff and her husband will lovingly tease her body until he *makes* her go over the edge into an orgasm of incredible pleasure.

If he controls her body by doing what he's found out will drive her wild, half of the wildness will be what he's doing to her body, and the other half will be that he's taken control and knows what to do.

That's what turns her on.

As long as two people stay sexually "in love", they will never part.

2
Taking Charge of Your Beloved's Body

The one thing every woman wants, craves, dreams of and hopes for, is a man who will take charge of her body. Not her money, not her diet, not her friends—but her body.

The way I found this and every other sex answer I needed was by doing sex surveys. They are difficult, expensive, and time-consuming to do, but because they're filled out anonymously (no names, addresses, phone numbers), they're very accurate.

When you have a person questioning you face to face, it's much more difficult (if not impossible) because of shyness or embarrassment, to get truthful answers

I first did a sex survey of 486 married women for my book about love, *Isle Of View (say it out loud!)*.

Then I did a sex survey of 1102 married women for my book *How To Satisfy A Woman*.

Next I did a sex survey of 510 married men for my book *How To Satisfy A Man*.

The last sex survey I did was of five hundred forty-nine married women in 2006/7. There were forty-five questions, and I found three of them (the same three I asked the five hundred ten married men) to be the most important and enlightening answers of all.

#41 was: "Would you like your husband to take sexual control of your body?"

#42 was: "Would you like to take sexual control of your husband's body?"

#43 was: "Would you like to take sexual control of each other's body?"

Those three questions were the only three in the survey that had 100% "yes" answers from both the men and women.

I wasn't surprised that the married men answered 100% "yes", but I was a little surprised that all the married women answered the same. I knew that *I* wanted my husband to take charge of my body and that some other women did too, but I didn't know that all women wanted their husbands to take charge of their bodies too.

It's so sexy to know that your spouse is in control of your sexual body, and is able to give you the intense pleasure of teasing foreplay that can go on for many minutes or even an hour, driving you wild just short of an orgasm.

And then, when he's ready (remember, he's in charge—you'll be in charge later!), he decides when to give you an orgasm.

There are some women who are afraid to surrender, afraid to give themselves totally to their husbands because they feel emotionally insecure. In order to surrender, a woman has to know, has to really *know* that she is loved. And if she doesn't, she will just lie there impassively and become detached from sex and from her husband.

41

I understand this because I was afraid of giving myself totally when I was first married years ago, and I think many women have felt this at one time or another.

In order to make sure your wife feels enough love from you for her to become really "hot", you must express it. Before you start making love, tell her sincerely that you love her with all your heart. Then tell her again.

After you've made her feel loved, and you start the ultimate foreplay, she will slowly begin her surrender (possibly her first), and it will be sexually exciting for both of you.

You will notice how much more relaxed and loving she will be toward you, and that's the real beginning of being "in love".

Many men with their anatomy have an easy time with quick, uncomplicated orgasms, and it's easy for many of them to have sex with anyone, loved or unloved. And because of this, many men don't always equate sex with love, and they don't always realize the incredible importance that love plays with many women and sex.

However, when it comes to his wife taking charge of his body, there is nothing in his life that is as exciting as the thought of a woman taking charge of his penis.

Remember, every man without exception in my survey of married men said they wanted their wives to take charge of their bodies. 100%.

And when the woman he wants to spend the rest of his life with, his wife, has taken charge of his penis, his excitement is thrilling to him.

Something which can take as little as ten minutes (sometimes less) that's a really super-exciting thing for his wife to do, is to give him a daily "blow job" (aka a BJ).

If you want a written guarantee from me that if you give him exciting sex every day he'll never cheat on you, just email me— naurahayden@aol.com—and I'll be happy to give it to you. After my two previous incredibly successful marriage manuals, I consider myself a "sexpert".

I've been on well over one thousand TV and radio shows since 1981 (plus doing lots of other things too), and have talked to many, many thousands of married men and women and they all agree with me that sex belongs in marriage, women want husbands to "take charge" and give orgasms, men want wives to pay attention to them and to take charge of their penises.

And believe me, with a daily ten minute delicious BJ, no man is going to be looking outside his marriage for any exciting sex if he's got it at home. Just because you are focusing on his penis for ten minutes with your lips and tongue (remember, no teeth!), a BJ orgasm has to be exciting to him.

One thing very important to wives—if the thought that his ejaculation (his "come") in your mouth has to be swallowed is too much for you, the moment he comes in your mouth, have a tissue in your other hand (or your bra or pocket), and wipe it from your tongue and lips onto the tissue. Or into your hand which you can wipe on your thigh (it dries fast), or a sheet or anywhere. You don't have to swallow it.

Very few women do, and I've asked many men about it and they don't really care if you do or don't swallow it. You love him and you've given him intense pleasure, and that's the most important thing to him.

Now let's start with the husband taking

charge of his wife's body. Remember, an orgasm is sexual surrender. And the only person you would surrender to is someone as powerful as, or more powerful than you, certainly no one weaker.

So when your husband takes charge of giving you an orgasm, he's also in charge of everything leading up to the orgasm. When he starts the ultimate foreplay, you will surrender to him almost totally, but not quite, which only comes with orgasm.

To be deeply in love is to feel like the love slave of your beloved.

But your beloved does not make you a love slave.

You make *yourself* a love slave—happily and willingly.

This power over you is something you consciously and willingly give (in your mind, heart and soul) to your beloved.

And when a wife takes charge of giving her husband's penis an orgasm, she's also in charge of everything leading up to his orgasm and he becomes her love slave.

It happens when both of you surrender to each other.

45

Men don't want affairs, they want to fall deeply in love just as women want. And each man deeply in love wants to be his wife's love slave just as his deeply-in-love wife wants to be his.

The only thing you need emotionally for this is the trust that comes from being *mutually* "in love".

Now if a wife or husband were always the love slave, it would eventually be boring because doing the same thing all the time is always boring. And of course if either one were always master, that also would be boring. So the answer is they take turns, depending on how they feel.

Whenever you take charge of your mate's body, you are definitely the master, and when your mate takes charge of your body, you are definitely the slave.

It's exciting either way—being master is fun and being love slave is fun.

The more fun in your marriage, the more fun your life will be.

As long as two people stay sexually "in love", they will never part.

3
EDTA &
Mind-blowing
Delicious Sex

There is something extremely important that I've discovered since I wrote my last book, and that is EDTA, which is Ethylene Diamine Tetra-acetic Acid.

<u>It is not a drug and there are no side effects.</u>

If your body doesn't feel sexy, if your sex organs—penis, clitoris, nipples—never (or hardly ever) get an urge to be touched, caressed, sucked, licked, or made love to, or when they are it doesn't drive you and your body wild and feel exciting and sexy, then you need EDTA.

Everyone who knows me or who has read any of my eight books knows that I am a "health nut", and won't put anything into my body unless it's healthy and/or health-giving. I don't take any drug or substance with side-effects, not even aspirin.

I've studied nutrition for years to find all the info I could about the different vitamins, minerals and nutraceuticals constantly being discovered and tested, and changed my body much for the better by changing my diet and taking all the good things I'd found out about.

I was very excited to be called by Congressman Fred Richmond to testify before the Congressional Committee on Nutrition, which was a great thrill for me.

Then I met the founder of the International Academy of Preventive Medicine, Dr. Richard Brennan, when we did a TV show together in Seattle, and he asked me to be the keynote speaker at their annual meeting in Dallas of over five hundred highly respected doctors from all over the world. When I returned to New York after the speech, I received a beautiful parchment document with my name inscribed on it, making me an Honorary Fellow of the International Academy of Preventive Medicine, which was another great thrill for me.

I only relate this to you so you'll know that I have some knowledge of foods, drugs, vitamins, minerals, etc.

EDTA is, again, not a drug, it's a substance that goes through your blood vessels (like a non-nutritive fiber) that cleans them, just like Roto-Rooter cleans out dirty, clogged-up pipes in your house.

It was discovered in the 1930s when many thousands of little kids were eating the lead paint that was peeling off the walls of tenements and older apartment houses. Science found that the only thing that went through their bodies and took with it the deadly lead was EDTA.

Over the years it has saved countless thousands of children from certain death.

EDTA is also called chelation, from the Greek word "chele" which means "claw", and what it does is grab any heavy metals, excess calcium, etc. in your blood stream or lining

49

your blood vessels, and it carries them out of your body.

EDTA is now used for other physical problems, and many of the EDTA treatments are done with a liquid form given intravenously in a doctor's office. It takes about an hour for the drip to be completed, is fairly expensive, starting at over $100. per treatment, and people usually take at least one and sometimes two a week.

But the EDTA pills are cheap and work slower but very well, and that's what I take — read on.

The first time I heard about EDTA was several years ago when I found out it's used primarily now for heart patients, again, as a blood vessel "Roto-Rooter" that goes through a body and gets rid of all the harmful substances that can cause a heart attack.

Then, when I was in Philadelphia doing a radio show at station WWDB-AM, and Irv Homer was the host, I really learned about EDTA. Irv is a dynamic talk show host who covered serious topics, has a great sense of humor, and is a super guy, and when I got to the studio early, he asked me to come in and listen to a live phoner he was doing with a guest he'd had on before.

The show was about heart problems and bypass surgeries It seems the guest had had several bypass surgeries and was due for another one when a friend of his suggested EDTA to clean out his clogged up blood vessels.

He tried the EDTA, un-clogged his blood vessels, and went back to his heart specialist who couldn't believe that simple chelation had made the bypass unnecessary.

Now the host, Irv Homer, also had heart problems and was also due to have open-heart surgery when the guest had last appeared on his show several months earlier.

Irv also tried EDTA and was able to cancel his bypass operation. I was stunned that something as simple and inexpensive as EDTA could obviate something as serious and tremendously expensive as open-heart surgery.

Then I started researching EDTA and found the data on children in the 30s dying of lead poisoning from peeling paint. I was intrigued that this simple, very inexpensive formula could heal two deadly physical problems.

In continuing my search I discovered an article about two forms of EDTA—again, the liquid form that's given intravenously that costs over $100. a treatment, and also a pill form that you swallow twice a day that costs about 3 cents each pill, or around $15.00 a bottle for two hundred fifty pills which last four months, ($3.75 a month), taking two a day.

The article explained how it does the same thing as the intravenous, only slower and much cheaper, as it cleans out veins and arteries of all the sludge (heavy metals such as lead, cadmium, barium, excessive iron, copper and aluminum, plus excessive calcium, etc.) and I decided to try it.

Now I've always been a sexy-feeling woman. In fact when I was a little girl, starting from about age ten on, I started having a special dream several times a week. On those mornings when I'd had the dream, I'd come in to breakfast with the family and always tell my mom and dad about how I'd flown off the front porch again.

Neither had a clue what I was talking

about nor commented on my dream, so I wondered about it for years, until I had my first orgasm. Then I knew what had happened. I guess it's like a boy having a wet dream, except there was no evidence of anything after my dream.

Going back to the EDTA, after about four or five weeks of taking it twice a day, I noticed I was getting to feel a little sexier than I'd felt for a while. And the longer I took it, the sexier I felt—and then after a little more time, I started to feel exceedingly sexy, and I love feeling that way.

As months went by I kept feeling sexier than ever. I couldn't believe how sensual my body had become, actually more than it had ever been.

The reason is that EDTA was cleaning out my body's blood vessels.

Our bodies are filled with veins and arteries taking blood through the body and returning it to the heart to be re-oxygenated.

It's not just our arms and legs, trunk, neck and head that have these veins and arteries. They're also in our sex organs. If our blood vessels are clogged with heavy metals, excess calcium, etc., our circulation of blood is slowed throughout our bodies.

Particularly in our sex organs.

When a man has ED, or erectile dysfunction, his obstructed penis blood vessels are unable to fill with blood, so they can't make it big and hard and ready to penetrate his beloved. But when he cleans out the clogged blood vessels with EDTA, his penis now can engorge with blood and get big and hard and give him and his wife enormous pleasure.

And of course the same with a woman's clitoris, her "mini-penis".

And her nipples.

When the veins and arteries are clogged in her clit and nipples, she cannot be aroused. You can suck her nipples, but it won't drive her wild and crazy. You can play with her clit, rub it, do anything you want with it and it won't excitingly respond. Not that it doesn't want to. It can't respond with the clogged blood supply.

And just like a husband's penis, when the blood vessels in her clit and nipples are un-clogged and engorge with blood, her sexual pleasure will overwhelm her.

To have a sexually receptive body for your beloved is what heaven is: two people in love who want to pleasure each other by making beautiful love with their sexual bodies and giving each other the ultimate pleasure of incredibly powerful orgasms.

I buy my EDTA from a company in Nashville which, again, costs $14.95 for two hundred fifty pills which you'll take twice a day and they last four months. Each pill costs about three cents, so it's six cents a day for two pills.

You can find out how and where to buy it on page 140 at the back of the book.

You take one EDTA tablet after breakfast or mid-morning and the other one after dinner or before you go to bed.

Because the EDTA depletes a small amount of vitamins and minerals at the same time it takes out the heavy metals and excess calcium deposits, you must take a vitamin/ mineral supplement (pages 142–143) with it after breakfast and dinner.

And remember, because it's the inexpensive oral chelation instead of the expensive intravenous, it takes more time to see and feel the results. But be patient, because you absolutely will feel the difference. Sometimes it takes a few weeks, and if your blood vessels are very clogged, it may take a little longer to get them totally clean. But in the interim your veins and arteries will be getting a little cleaner and you'll be feeling a little sexier every day.

EDTA is for women and men. We all need to clean out our bodies, to get rid of all the gunk obstructing our blood vessels, which is the reason we stop feeling sexy in the first place.

Again, a man's penis and his wife's clitoris and nipples, are aroused *only* when the blood vessels of both are engorged with blood. And this can *only* happen when the blood vessels are not clogged with the heavy metals, an excess of calcium, cholesterol, etc. And EDTA will do it.

Something also very important is that there are substances that are "orgasm blockers" that strongly affect women, (I cover "potency blockers" that affect men in my *How To Satisfy A Man* book).

These "orgasm blockers" are cigarettes,

which dilate all your blood vessels, particularly those in a woman's clitoris and nipples (and of course a man's penis), plus caffeine, hormonal birth control, sugar, stress, anti-depressants, and many other legal and illegal drugs.

Some very good substances which help women's bodies to be more orgasmic, are any and all fruits and veggies which keep the body alkaline, (which is what the body wants and needs), whereas sugar and all animal products make the body acid, (which is what the body *doesn't* want). Plus the "feel good" neurotransmitter, dopamine, and another brain chemical, serotonin, need to be alkaline to keep a woman relaxed and feeling good, and without them, her body will be filled with tension and/or depression. .

I work very hard at being healthy for a good reason—I used to be not-healthy, and had terrible depressions. At that time I did a lot of things that made me unhealthy and made a lot of extra health problems for me.

I started smoking a pack of cigs a day at 18 and quit in my 30s when I finally realized how bad it was for me. And at the same time I drank a lot of alcohol and used a lot of uppers, downers, grass and other drugs (I sure wish I hadn't done that then). Plus I ate way too much sugar every day (in my coffee, pancake syrup, donuts, candy bars, ice cream, etc.) I'm a "cause & effect" person, and I've learned how bad sugar is with its deadly addictive effects.

Working at being healthy really pays off. I feel better now than I've ever felt, and as time goes on I keep feeling better every day.

I take lots of vites and mins, and eat really healthy food. I don't eat any sugar at all, and lots of fruits and veggies. I drink mucho water and I'm a vegan.

I used to be a vegetarian, ate no meat or fish because I am against killing of any thing, but I ate lots of eggs, cheese, yogurt, and drank a quart of milk every day. As my clogged-up sinus got worse, I decided to cut out the milk and see what happened, and when my sinus cleared up I stopped using any milk.

Soon after I gave up yogurt, cheese and eggs and became a total vegan, and my health is now so fantastic it's worth never tasting scrambled eggs, chocolate soufflés, or ice cream (used to be my all-time favorite food I would choose to have on a desert island if I could only have one food 24/7).

Also I used to love all cheeses, particularly camembert and cottage cheese, plus custard, and stuffed hard boiled eggs.

But now, no dairy.

The best book ever written about food (and I've been reading books about food and nutrition since my mid-twenties) is "The China Study" by T. Colin Campbell, a scientist at Cornell University. It's fairly new, and if you really want to cure yourself of most illnesses, read this book and change your life much for the better.

He covers cancer, heart problems, brain problems, diabetes, osteoporosis—no matter what the disease, his book tells what causes the problems (you will probably be very surprised to find out what causes osteoporosis— I sure was!). Because he's a brilliant scientist he did enormous studies in the Phillipines, India and China, where he found the answers to healing the most perplexing human diseases. It's a great, easy-to-read, incredibly interesting book.

I don't eat any wheat either because I found that wheat clogs my intestines (and you know what *that* means!), and nothing is worth that. Pasta used to be my second-favorite food (after ice cream), and I miss angel hair cappellini with olive oil and fresh garlic (I can still taste it).

Everybody has a different chemical balance or imbalance, and something that bothers me may not necessarily bother you, and vice versa. However, if some food does bother me, it's likely it might bother you and lots of other people too.

Many people have said to me that life isn't worth living without the foods I chose to stop eating, but I totally disagree. Life is so much better without tension, anxiety and/or depression. Plus the intense pleasure of sex more than takes the place of foods I've given up.

And very logically, we'll turn that around so we can see that the pleasure of addictive sugar-laden foods sadly takes the place of the non-existent sex in one's life.

One of my all-time favorite adages is **"You can have anything in life you want—**

it all depends on what you're willing to give up for it." And I'm willing to give up anything that makes me tense, nervous, anxious and/or depressed!

I've found that people who are addicted to, or sensitive to, cigs, booze, drugs, sugar, wheat, etc., and continue using them, don't have happy sex lives. In fact, most don't have any kind of sex life at all.

This isn't a guess—it's a definite answer. While writing my other two marriage manuals and doing the in-depth surveys, I had the opportunity to ask men and women intimate questions about their sex lives, about their eating habits, and if they have any addictions.

And all of those with non-existent sex lives (or sex lives with little or no love, or few or no orgasms) have to put something into their lives that they find pleasure-full and/or exciting, and food is the closest thing to physical pleasure they've found.

Others find that alcohol, cigarettes and other drugs happily (for them) dull the senses, which also dulls the pain of unhappy love lives and sex lives.

In almost every book I've written I have listed all the vites and mins I take every day—I've done that because I sincerely believe that if everyone takes care of their bodies as I do mine, they will be as healthy as I am, and feel as good as I do.

And because I was in such bad shape physically and mentally (terrible depressions with suicidal tendencies) and know the horror of not wanting to live anymore, I feel qualified to try to get everyone to change their chemical imbalances as I did mine. These terrible depressions were only before I stopped eating bad foods and started taking vitamins, and now I never get depressed and always feel incredibly great.

It's as easy to pop a couple of vitamin pills as it is a couple of prescription drugs, and many, many millions of people do the drugs their doctors prescribe and don't bitch about not having time to take them like some people bitch about vitamins. Well, the vites don't have any negative side effects and can possibly keep you from ever having to take the drugs. They've done that for me.

I list on pages 142–143 which vitamins

and minerals I take, and how much I take every day.

But I would also like to mention several things I've found since my last book that have helped me immensely to feel terrific, and I buy them regularly. I list on pages 140–141 in the back of the book the places you can find all these great products.

One (besides the EDTA which is listed) is Natural Calm, a wonderful product made in L.A. that I discovered several years ago when the company sent me (and probably many thousands of other people) samples of it. It's a magnesium powder and magnesium is missing in many people's diets, so it restores healthy levels of it to regulate your body.

Natural Calm is very good to take before bedtime to help you sleep, and also (like Milk of Magnesia) helps to regulate your intestines. Except this is a highly absorbable special formula of pH-balanced magnesium citrate in ionic form. Which is a lot of words to tell you it's a great formula.

Again, Natural Calm, as the name implies, helps to keep you relaxed and free of tension.

Several years ago I discovered coconut oil

when I read on the web that coconut oil fats are very similar to fats in mother's milk, and have the same nutraceutical effect. It's extremely healthy because, when eaten, the lauric acid in coconut oil (and mother's milk) forms monolaurin which destroys bacteria and viruses in babies and adults.

But on top of all that, the taste of coconut oil is so good, and putting it in oatmeal, yams, salads, etc., gives them a slight coconut flavor, which I happen to love. So I use it every day in different foods I make. And read on page 96 how else I use it deliciously.

And after I started using the coconut oil, I found out the same company makes noni juice (made from noni fruit) which I'd read is a natural detoxifier which boosts the immune system, alkalinizes the body and helps the intestines get rid of waste and toxins. It's tart with a strong tarty taste.

I tried it, loved it, and take it straight from the bottle first thing every morning (most people take it in juice). I'll take anything <u>natural</u> if there's a chance I'll feel even better than I do already

I try everything that makes sense, and if

I don't get a great body reaction, I don't use it again, but if I like it and feel a real difference, I take it every day. I drink my noni juice every morning and love it.

In fact I liked both the coconut oil and noni juice so much that I called the company to compliment them on their great products (I do things like that!). After a long conversation they wanted to make a deal to handle the business end of my products (I'm not a whiz in the biz world!), and I just recently did that. Not only are their products great, the people are too.

Next is a product I've been taking for many years—GH3. I found out about it through the late Herbert Bailey whom I met in 1970 and who became a very close friend. He was a brilliant nutrition researcher who wrote eight books in the health sciences.

I was doing Barry Farber's terrific radio show on WOR-AM in New York City and I mentioned a book, "Vitamin E, Your Key To A Healthy Heart" by Herbert Bailey as a must-read for every one listening.

A friend of his heard the show and told Herb, who called the station, left a message and I called him the next day. We met and stayed close friends for many years.

One day he took me to meet Dr. Ana Aslan, a cardiologist who later became a gerontologist and was a national heroine in her country, Romania, because of her work with the very powerful GH3.

She had come to New York for some international medical meetings, and had become a friend of Herbie's on her previous visit. He was now doing a new book about GH3 and wanted to interview her, which he did in her hotel room with me in tow.

She was seventy-eight but looked and acted much younger, and had a cute little figure. She didn't actually discover GH3, but she was the first person to discover its use as an anti-depressant and an anti-aging substance with no side effects.

I was fascinated as she and Herb discussed how and why GH3 works. There exists in the brain of every human body monoamine oxidase (MAO) which is an enzyme, and around the age of forty-five (sometimes as young as the mid-thirties, but *always* by forty-five) MAO begins to build up and increase in the brain, displacing other vital substances.

One of these displaced substances, norepinephrine (noradrenaline), is a hormone essential to our vitality and sense of well-being, and it was found that real aging and age-related depression begins around the time MAO starts its buildup in our mid-forties.

Now scientists have known for many years that suppressing MAO with drugs could cure depression and lessen the symptoms of aging, but they found that all the drugs tried were irreversible inhibitors of MAO, and anything that permanently destroys MAO is dangerous because it's necessary to maintain the homeostasis of the body (it regulates blood pressure, protects the liver, etc.).

Dr. Aslan found that GH3 temporarily inhibits MAO and allows it to return when needed. GH3 also increases the level of serotonin (an important and essential brain amine), and allows it to coexist with noradrenaline in the brain.

This amazing product is made with

Procaine, but when it's buffered with benzoic acid, potassium metabisulfite and disodium phosphate, it becomes GH3 which is a "Pro-Vitamin", or "Vitamin Precursor". GH3 breaks down in the body to help form different vitamins—folic acid, choline, acetylcholine, plus naturally occurring compounds including the powerful DEAE (diethylaminoethanol) and PABA (para-aminobenzoic acid, a B vitamin). DEAE then breaks down into DMAE (dimethylaminoethanol) which is widely known to be a brain function enhancer.

I was so excited to be in the midst of a conversation with the woman who started it all that I asked her if she thought I should begin to take GH3 even though I was not yet forty-five, and she said "Only if you want to stay young and not be depressed." I started!

But at that time you could only get it in Europe, and I used to mail-order it in either Switzerland or Romania. The FDA had outlawed it being made in the U.S. (the reason was that the drug companies put the pressure on D.C. because with GH3 you don't need a prescription like you do for all the very expensive anti-depressant drugs).

Fortunately for all of us, a friend of mine I met long after I started taking GH3, Rodger Sless, went to court about it, and after much time and money, he actually won. We were all happily stunned that Rodger beat the multi-billion dollar drug companies, and now it's being made in the U.S.

I list in the back of the book (page 141) where you can buy it just as I do. It's fairly inexpensive, $108. for a six month supply of GH3—$18. a month, or 25 cents twice a day.

It must be taken on an empty stomach, two hours after food and one hour before your next food. I take mine anywhere between 3:30 and 5:30 A.M. in the morning when I get up to go to the bathroom but am not up yet for the day, and it seems to relax my brain and puts me back to sleep. Then my second GH3 pill I take around 5:00 P.M. in the afternoon, two or more hours after lunch and one or more hours before dinner. Thank you, Herbert Bailey!

As I was writing this story about GH3, there was an article on *WebMD* by Miranda Hitti of *WebMD Medical News* (reviewed by

Louise Chang, MD) about an international study done on depression with over two hundred thousand people in seventy two countries.

USA TODAY had the same story.

Two researchers, one from Great Britain, Andrew Oswald, and the other from the USA, David Blanchflower, analyzed data on human depression from more than thirty-five years, and "they found that men and women in their forties were more likely to be depressed . . . for both sexes, the probability of depression peaks around age forty-four." And they stated they don't have any idea why this happens.

This is how well the knowledge about GH3 has been suppressed and kept hidden from almost everyone, and I hope that both of the researchers read this book and find out about MAO (monoamine oxidase) and the incredible GH3.

Over twenty-five years ago I formulated my own Dynamite Energy Shake and Dynamite Vites, which I take every single day, the Shake for breakfast with three Vites, and then three Vites later after dinner. These are also listed in the back of the book on page 141. All profits which go to me I put in The John Ellsworth Hayden Foundation, named after my late father, which gives free Dynamite Energy Shakes to people who need great nutrition but can't buy it—people in government facilities: prisons, old-age homes, mental health institutions, etc.

I formulated the DES for my own body in 1981 because I couldn't find any product that gave me the amount of vitamins, minerals and protein that I wanted and felt I needed. I put in more of just about everything, and it works 'cause I have more energy than anybody I ever met.

There are two nutrients I take every day with my Dynamite Energy Shake & Dynamite Vites: CoQ10, an antioxidant that produces energy within all your cells (particularly the heart and liver), and Ginkgo Biloba, which increases blood flow supplying oxygen and nutrients to the brain, helping the memory and thinking ability

All these things that I take help to make me feel as great as I do, and I'll take them for the rest of my life.

The bottom line is that to be in love and

have exciting delicious sex and a great marriage, you both need to take care of your bodies and eat only healthful, nourishing food. And take certain vitamins, minerals and nutraceuticals that science has proved our bodies need to stay healthily active.

And most importantly, that our bodies need to stay romantically and sexually active with our spouses.

As long as two people stay sexually "in love", they will never part.

4
For Men Who *Really* Love Their Wives

A man who truly loves his wife truly wants to do whatever he can to make her happy. That's what being in love is all about. And having a sexually delicious marriage will make both of them happy.

To make this happen takes focus. You must realize that if you are able to bring your wife sexual excitement (which automatically makes you sexually excited), nothing can ever come between the two of you.

I'm going to repeat myself here, but the very important thing every man should learn (and I don't think too many men know) is that the first step to great lovemaking is love. It may not sound new or true—you may be thinking I'm grossly exaggerating the importance of love, (you know how women get!).

But a married woman needs to feel loved in order to feel really sexy. She needs to know her husband truly loves her so she will be able to relax enough to surrender to him and trust him not to hurt her emotionally in any way.

Because a man's sex organs are for the most part on the outside of his body (and hers for the most part are on the inside), it's much easier for him to orgasm than it is for his wife.

And because a woman's mini-penis is so much smaller than his maxi job, it's that much more difficult for her to have an orgasm.

Besides that, most women are not able to surrender sexually to someone they don't love, someone they fear, or if they feel unloved by a person. They are only able to surrender sexually to someone they love and trust, someone they feel also loves them.

And how does a woman know her husband loves her?

By his telling her.

Some men have the notion the wife should realize that because he goes to work every day to earn money for her and the family, that this should tell her that he loves her.

Of course she realizes he's working for her and the family, and of course she loves him for it. But how does she know he still really deeply loves her?

Perhaps she thinks that he could be bored and maybe looking around. She needs to hear him tell her of his love before she can feel emotionally and sexually secure.

So if he's sensitive at all to his wife's emotional needs, he will know she has to hear him say "Honey, I love you", "Baby, I'm crazy about you", "Sweetheart, I love you more than anything in the world".

THAT'S what I'm talking about.

And not just when they make love (although that's a really great and important time to tell her how much you love her), I'm talking during the day calling her just to tell her you love her.

I learned at a very young age that not all men are expressive. Some men have a very tough time being expressive. Their nature is to be super-masculine, and to them, that means not romantic.

Well, my belief is that if these non-expressive men really love their wives and truly want them to be happy and to have happy marriages, they can condition themselves to be more and more loving in their marriages.

Every time one of them says "I love you, Baby", it makes a notch in his brain, and the more notches, the easier it becomes. It's like any habit. Do it enough and it becomes second nature to do it.

And there are many men who are afraid of intimacy, who hold back their emotions, who are petrified of surrendering to any woman, including their wives (believe me, I know).

If a man values his wife and his marriage at all, he'll try marriage counseling, he'll read books, he'll try anything to figure out what his problem is and how he can overcome it.

But it is overcomeable. It might not be easy, and it might have to be "fought for".

Many things worthwhile in life are not really easy, but the rewards for overcoming adversity, for honestly trying to change yourself for the better and slowly succeeding with self-discipline and determination, are sweet and make you feel so good about yourself that they are definitely worth the time and effort.

I've had many love relationships and the only reason some of them lasted till death did us part, was that my husband or fiance or boyfriend told me every day how much he loved me.

And my joy at hearing this overflowed into "I love you too, Darling." And of course I also was many times first to tell him how much I loved him, and he always responded lovingly.

Every man wants his wife to be happy. They would still be dating and he wouldn't have married her if he didn't truly love her, and love begets happiness.

And of course there's not a man alive married to a woman he's in love with who wouldn't do anything to make sure his wife is sexually satisfied.

When I went around the country promoting my *How To Satisfy A Woman* book you might be surprised (I was!) how many women called me on radio shows and said that all men are selfish and only want their own sexual satisfaction.

That is totally untrue. Any man who loves a woman enough to marry her would do anything to give her an orgasm.

He just doesn't know how.

And he sure doesn't know how to get her excited enough in foreplay so she's panting with passion to have an orgasm.

The only reason it appears that men are selfish is that too many men, after a minute or so of foreplay (when they believe their wives are burning up with desire for them), put it in and start pumping forcefully (they think that pumping hard makes their wives even hotter), and their ignorance turns their wives off sex altogether.

The thing every wife in the world wants is for her husband to know what to do to make her hot in the first place. She wants her husband to know how to excite her, what parts of her body she'd love him to touch.

She doesn't want to have to tell him "A little to the right", "down a little bit", "a little higher", etc.

She would give anything if her husband would take charge of her body (which every woman wants her husband to do), and make her hot as a pistol and ready to have an orgasm.

It's not easy for him to know how different our sexual bodies feel. How would he know that what feels great to him doesn't always feel great to her? Who would have told him that? The kids on the block as he was growing up? His mother? His father? His teacher?

His wife knows that he's doing it all wrong, that it doesn't drive her crazy with desire, but she doesn't know what to tell him to do that's right.

And she'd give anything if he would learn on his own how to make her quiver with desire for him.

If women all over the world knew what to tell their husbands to do to make them have incredible pleasure and then orgasms, we wouldn't have fights, separations, affairs, divorces, etc.

A man can't fake it because it's apparent when he has an orgasm—he ejaculates sperm, but with a woman there's no proof that she's climaxed. And faking it is so easy.

Some people point out that her nipples get hard when she has an orgasm (women have different bodies and some act and react differently), but her nipples also may get hard when she's aroused. And getting aroused isn't difficult.

She gets aroused lying nude next to him, praying that he's going to take charge of her body and make her hot and then make her have an orgasm. The thought of having an orgasm is just as exciting to a woman as it is to a man.

Women do get aroused, but the difficulty can be that he doesn't know how to make her *greatly* aroused or how to make love once she is aroused. And because of this, she'll never know sexually delicious sex and she'll never fall "in love" with him.

The ultimate foreplay, if her nipples and clit are sexually responsive (CH 3), will make her burn up and sizzle with heat!

Now some men may say that what I'm

suggesting to do is much too much time and work. But if you really do want to turn your marriage around and really do want to put some excitement into it, you have to do *something* to make that happen.

When you work for a company, any company, from Ford Motor Company to Nabisco to the U.S. Government, or even if you own your own biz, you know how you have to focus and how you have to work really hard to make a living.

Well, your marriage is actually much more important than anything else in your life. You can always find another job but you can't always find the right love partner to spend the rest of your life with.

You found your wife and fell in love with her, and the most important thing is to make sure she's emotionally and sexually happy so that your marriage will grow into a haven of deep love for both of you.

As long as two people stay sexually "in love", they will never part.

5
For Women Who *Really* Love Their Husbands

The most important thing about men that women don't understand is how depressed a man gets if his sex life has gotten seriously boring.

It may seem foolish to a woman that the lack of exciting sex can cause real depression in a man's life, but his need for sexual excitement is so important that without it, some men actually feel they don't want to get up in the morning and don't want to go to work. They're so depressed they can't function well.

And all it takes is some hot babe at work, or at the bar, or on the bus (the places he could meet her would more than fill this page), to bring him out of his depression.

And when it comes to a man actually cheating on his wife, a woman doesn't understand that a man doesn't cheat because another woman is younger or prettier, he cheats because sex becomes so boring when his wife starts ignoring his penis and focuses on the kids, the house, her job, her pals, but not on his penis.

To a man, his penis is responsible for his mental, emotional, spiritual and physical well-being. Now not every man is fully aware of this, but he does know his penis is extremely important to his life.

If you pay attention to his sexual needs he will feel loved and sexually satisfied, and won't need to fool around.

Ever since years ago when I found out my second husband was cheating (my first husband died), and I analyzed it to try to figure out why he was fooling around, I began to understand that I had become complacent.

This was long before I discovered my

technique, and sex with him was not too thrilling. But even though I wasn't "in love" with him, I did love him and didn't want the marriage to end. But infidelity is a no-no, and I ended it.

But I finally figured out that I was the one at fault.

It was because I wasn't paying attention to him or to his penis. And because of the insights I gained through my own self-analysis, I became aware that what led to the divorce was my inattention.

Any wife who puts her husband second to her kids, house, pals, job, etc., will always be responsible for her husband's cheating. And of course the opposite is also true—if a husband puts his wife second to his job, his pals, his kids, he'll be responsible if she cheats on him.

Most men are different from most women—a man needs sexual excitement every day of his life.

He doesn't have to have actual physical sex every day (however, that's the ultimate thrill for him), it can be just the thought of someone who turns him on.

84

And the thought of his sexy wife will do it.

And you will be sexy (oh yeah!) once he gets to the ultimate foreplay with you.

I have often likened a man's need for sexual excitement to a diabetic's need for insulin. If you give a diabetic a daily dose of insulin, the diabetes is controlled and he is healthy. If you give a man a daily dose of oral sex, his need for sexual excitement is controlled and the marriage thrives.

If you don't give the insulin, the man dies of diabetic coma. And if you don't pay attention and focus on the man's penis, the marriage dies of marital coma.

When a man is happy sexually at home and truly satisfied by his wife, no woman can seduce him.

Men are usually only aware of sexual attractions and sexual feelings and not aware that "falling in love" begins as a sexual attraction, and the sexual pull must be there or he can't and won't fall in love.

In my surveys of married men and women, I asked lots of interesting questions, and one for the man was about why he was first attracted to his wife. Was it because he thought she was a sweet person? Did he like her personality? Did he think she'd make a great mother? Was it her face, eyes, hair? Did he think she was sexy?

Almost every one answered he was attracted because he thought she was sexy. Although one fellow did say he thought she'd make a terrific mother (he answered "no" to two of my questions asking if he or his wife is happily married).

As long as a man is in love he'll stay sexually excited, and as long as he's sexually excited, he'll stay in love.

Once a man has made the decision that your body and soul are the only body and soul that he wants to merge his body and soul with, he is in love.

And once you let him down and don't keep his body and soul excited with the promise of great body and soul-exploding sex on a constant basis, he will make the decision (consciously or unconsciously) to fall out of love with you.

He will probably still love you if you still love him, but he won't be "in love" with you anymore. And he will probably still need you to take care of some of his needs; that is, he'll need you until he finds a woman who excites him sexually.

The one absolutely, positively infallible way to keep his life with you exciting is to give him sexually exciting, delicious sex.

Another important fact for every wife is that men under stress (and who isn't under stress nowadays?) are prone to heart attacks, and sex is a wonderful and healthy way for her to make sure her husband doesn't have one.

Dr. Eugene Scheimann, author of *Sex Can Save Your Heart and Life,* states that sex also makes us physically healthier:

Sex is the best and cheapest remedy for emotional stress.

Sex is excellent exercise and effective therapy.

Sex helps prevent hormone imbalance and reduces the narrowing of coronary arteries.

Sex reduces the cholesterol level.

Sex helps ease the frustrations of "coronary risks" who are then less

87

likely to eat, drink or smoke to excess.

Sex often assures a happier, more harmonious family life. Heart attacks are 50% more frequent among unmarried men.

Sex for older men prevents impotency, masculinity crisis, and the "menopausal syndrome".

Sex for women satisfies basic needs—and sex can slow down the aging process.

Sex invites tenderness and togetherness, and discourages hostility, self destruction and loneliness.

Sex and love provide hope, optimism and a positive state of mind and well-being—crucial factors in the treatment of heart and other stress-related diseases.

So now you and your mate can give each other intense, sexually delicious pleasure as often as you like, (hopefully maybe every day) and know you're also keeping each other a lot healthier.

There's a sexual fact about a woman's

body that I think should be understood by everyone: a man must have an orgasm in order to procreate a child. But a wife can literally have ten children and never have an orgasm—so her clitoris is there for one reason, and one reason *only*—to give her pleasure with her husband.

I believe the reason that this pleasure bond is so intense is to make sure the wife stays with her mate. And she will, once he learns how to make her body so hot she'll never look at another man.

Why would she? The man she loves and is married to gives her the greatest sexual pleasure she's ever had, and will continue as long as they're together.

As long as two people stay sexually "in love", they will never part.

6
The Ultimate Sexual Foreplay

Foreplay has almost always been a prelude to the "main event", intercourse. But now, I've made the ultimate sexual foreplay a very powerful sexual "event" all by itself. This arousal of sexual excitement in a woman may or may not end in intercourse, it may last for thirty minutes or even longer, but it definitely will drive her body wild with desire.

One of my favorite really exciting sexy love songs that reminds me of what "in love" is really all about is *That Old Black Magic,* music by Harold Arlen with lyrics by Johnny

Mercer. It became a huge hit and eventually a "standard" because it brilliantly captures the excitement of delicious "in love" sex. Here are a few lyrics of how it feels when you first fall in love:

> ". . . Icy fingers up and down my spine, the same old witchcraft when your eyes meet mine . . .

> . . . I hear your name and I'm aflame, A flame with such a burning desire That only your lips can put out the fire.

> . . . Every time your lips meet mine, Darling . . . round and round I go in a spin, loving the spin I'm in . . ."

That's exactly how I've felt the few times I've been deeply in love. Johnny Mercer's been there too!

And in order to make your love-making that spine-tingling, body-quivering, earth-shaking event, the very first thing you must again remember is that love is the bottom line of all truly great sexual pleasures. Sex without love can feel good. Sex with love is nirvana.

Love is the beginning aphrodisiac—the first step to being "in love" and sexual surrender.

Of course all sexual activity gives us pleasure and there's no such thing as an orgasm that doesn't feel good.

But when you and your beloved are truly deeply in love, so much so that you want to be together for a lifetime, and you get married, the sexual part of the marriage will be overwhelmingly pleasure-full once you learn the power of a sexual turn-on.

And this sexual foreplay is the most exciting sexual stimulant that a woman will have ever experienced. It's so powerful that it's the ultimate arousal that turns a woman's body on . . . and on . . . and on . . . and on . . .

Once a man learns how to give his wife the most intense *teasing* of her body, which eventually leads to the most intense orgasm she's ever had, both of them will do anything to please each other day or night just to guarantee the continuation of the constant arousal he creates for her body, which also greatly arouses him.

This sexual turn-on that he creates within her body makes her wait anxiously till he returns from the office/construction site/out-of-town-trip so she can hug him/kiss him/rub against his body, which is also a giant turn-on to him.

I'm sure that some feminists are by now gnashing their teeth and planning to picket bookstores with big signs.

I write this from an experience with my first marriage manual, when a bunch of feminists in San Francisco picketed a Barnes & Noble bookstore in 1982 because of the title *How To Satisfy a Woman Every Time . . . and have her beg for more!*

The problem with a few feminists is they have little sense of humor (I wish they had Ellen DeGeneres' sense of humor!), and of course ". . . and have her beg for more!" I liked 'cause I found it very amusing. But they didn't find it amusing, so they picketed the bookstore. Now *that's* amusing!!!

This new sexual technique is the ultimate foreplay. It will not only turn a woman on, it will keep her aroused on a constant basis till she has an orgasm.

And after she has an orgasm, she'll want her man to start turning her on again. And the more her husband turns her on, the more she craves it And the more he's turned on!

Married women have always known how their husbands would love to have certain parts of their bodies caressed, kissed, licked and sucked.

But married men have never known how their wives would love to have certain upper parts of their bodies caressed, kissed, licked and sucked lovingly longer than thirty or sixty seconds—how they'd adore it, go crazy for it.

But married women have never known it either.

Because they've never had it done for over sixty seconds. Oh, I know guys give perfunctory kisses on different parts of their wives' bodies, but they've never done "the real deal" which I'm writing about now.

Once a woman has these particular parts of her upper body sucked the right way (is there a wrong way—yes!), for ten minutes or a half hour, she'll never be the same. It's the most electrifying experience a woman's body can ever know.

For a woman to know that the man she loves, her husband, is going to take charge of her body and make it quiver in anticipation of what she knows is coming, is very exciting. And then when she feels the actual touch of his hand, his lips, his tongue on her body— this will bring her the most intense sexual pleasure she's ever known.

There's a very important part of this new sexual excitement—her mate must focus *totally* on turning his wife on.

This unselfishness on his part shows his wife how much he does truly love her by putting her pleasure above his own.

Even if he feels so sexy he'd like to mount her right away, he has to rise above this and continue arousing her. His time will come soon.

At the beginning, he must focus just on her body. He'll find that as she starts moaning/writhing/twisting, he'll be turned on just knowing the power he has over her body. And he'll find it is a giant turn-on.

One very important thing to have somewhere on the bed when you know you're going to make love is a jar of coconut oil, which I mentioned earlier.

It tastes great and has a fragrance of coconut that I love on some food, and because it's also very healthy it makes me feel I'm doing something good for my body.

One day the thought just popped into my head to use it sexually, and I have found it is the greatest, slipperiest, most fragrant, healthiest lubricant for any sexual play between the spouses. It smells good, tastes good, is good. You will literally love it.

If it's above 76 degrees F it will be oil, and if it's under 76 degrees F it will be hardened, but it liquefies almost immediately in your hand.

On page 140 at the back of the book, I list where you can buy the best extra-virgin coconut oil that I use.

The first thing you both do is lie nude next to each other, and you, her husband, wrap your arms around her and tell her how much you love her.

You'll feel her start to open herself to you

because knowing how much you love her will turn her on and make her want to give her self and her body to you, the man she knows and loves and trusts.

Remember, you can't totally surrender to someone you don't love or trust.

Next, you take your arms from around her, and slide down a bit in the bed till your head is opposite her breasts. You slowly and gently put your lips on one of her nipples and softly suck it. Very softly suck it, teasing it. Very loving, soft and gentle.

There is a direct line from her nipple to her clitoris, and while you're gently sucking and teasing her tit, her clit is becoming very hot.

As you're softly sucking her nipple, teasing it very gently, she's going very crazy, and you take your hand and dip it in the coconut oil jar, take a small amount of the oil (which absorbs into her skin fairly quickly), and gently rub her butt, gently rub her thighs, her tummy, her back, never stopping softly, gently sucking her nipple.

Of course you can arouse her greatly without anything, so try it without, but the coconut oil is soooooooo sexy.

Continue sucking her nipple gently, once in a while softly rubbing your tongue on her nipple in your mouth.

Keep softly massaging her body with the coconut oil (it feels incredibly sexy to her) as long as you can, never stopping your sucking her nipple. It could be for ten or fifteen minutes or even a half hour, just keep driving her sexually wild.

You have a choice of what you can do—if it's early morning and you or both of you have to go to work, tell her you'll turn her on again as soon as the two of you find a moment of time to make love again.

Trust me, she'll find some time sooner than you think. Her body will be craving your body. That's how intense the feeling of your lips on her nipple is.

She'll be thinking about it, re-playing the pleasure in her mind over and over again and thinking about how much she loves you for making her feel so incredibly sexy.

If it's a weekend and you have lots of time, continue gently sucking her tit and softly moving your oiled hand all over her body—

again, rub her butt, her hips, her tummy, her back, as she moans, letting you know how intense the pleasure is.

After a while of gently sucking her nipple and softly rubbing her body, you can slowly move your oiled hand down between her legs till your two fingers (index finger and middle finger) find her clit, that tiny little mini-penis sticking up, never taking your lips from her nipple. You'll be gently teasing her nipple and her clit (don't touch her clit hard, just softly *tease* it), and she'll be writhing on the bed, close to ecstasy.

You can take a little more coconut oil on your fingers, and while sucking her nipple, give her an orgasm with your fragrant oily two fingers very gently playing with and softly teasing her clit—you are now totally in charge and she loves it.

And make sure you find that little "bump", her mini-penis, and very gently tease "it" with your two fingers, and don't let your hand wander off "it" and go elsewhere. Keep softly sucking her tit, and gently teasing her clit, driving her crazy till she totally surrenders and has an orgasm.

The whole point of the "ultimate foreplay" is to very gently, very softly suck her nipple till she screams for mercy.

Believe me, I've been there and know how incredibly powerful this foreplay event is. And I do scream for mercy! It's overwhelmingly exciting.

Just be sure to gently suck her nipple and tease her clit. Don't get carried away with your own excitement of wanting to make love. Don't start sucking or rubbing too hard—her nipple and clit are *very* sensitive and you don't want to turn her off.

Plus whenever you're teasing her nipple, you're also teasing her clit.

If she moans a little louder and writhes a little more on the bed, you know you're right on target. If so, keep sucking her tit softly and gently. Believe me, if she wants it harder, she'll push her breast up to let you know she wants more. *Then, only then,* can you suck her nipple a little harder.

As a woman who's experienced it, I can tell you it's the greatest sexual pleasure I've ever had. The intensity of the pleasure is so strong that sometimes it's too much for me

100

and I have to pull my body away for just a moment till I regain my senses, and then the soft nipple-sucking begins again.

The love generated between a husband, who is showing his wife how much he loves her and is in charge of her body by giving her this incredible pleasure, and his wife showing him how much she loves him for giving her this intense pleasure, is overwhelmingly sensual to both of them.

Again, by putting his wife sexually first before he has any physical pleasure himself shows her how much he really does love her. And she will know this and love him deeply for his total unselfishness in giving her this intense sexual pleasure.

Now if you, her husband, are totally turned on by her moaning and writhing, and feel the time has come for your body inside hers, you can start the intercourse technique till her ecstasy is complete in her surrender to you in orgasm, followed by yours.

You will make your wife have an orgasm <u>every</u> <u>single</u> <u>time</u>—with intercourse alone— guaranteed! And making love that extra- special exciting teasing way will tease you too and make you extra sexy, so that your orgasm will be *much* more intense too.

It's very, very important that a man use this sexually powerful foreplay only with a woman he's in love with and married to. That's why this book is a marriage manual and not for unmarried people, and certainly not to be used on just a casual acquaintance or someone you just met.

It can be dangerous to fool around with a woman's emotions by giving her incredible sex.

So when a man goes to a single's bar and picks up a woman who doesn't turn him on enough to want to fall in love with (but her body's enough for him to want to "boff") and he goes with her to her place, has sex, and uses this sexually powerful foreplay in this book, she will go out of her mind with pleasure.

And she will believe he must love her to have driven her so wild with passion, and she will then and there fall in love with him.

What to him was a one-night-stand will become for her a love affair. She will either have her heart broken, which is terrible for her, or she'll become a stalker, which is terrible for him.

Sex, incredible sex, mind-blowing sex is the most powerful emotion in a person's life, and should be used only with great love in a faithful, loving, committed marriage.

As long as two people stay sexually "in love", they will never part.

7
Tone Your Body/ Build Your Muscles—in Bed

In order to have incredibly exciting sex in your life, you'd better have a body that responds to sexual feelings (after you take the EDTA, CH 3). And the best place to do this is in bed as soon as you wake up in the morning.

I started doing these exercises in my mid-twenties because I read an article about how much your body needs to be supple, and it gave some exercises that it said would accomplish that.

And once in a while I'd read about some

other exercise to limber up your torso, and I'd start doing that one too.

Whenever I read about something that I think would be really good for me and make me a healthier, smarter, nicer, all-around better person, I always at least try it. Sometimes I don't like it and don't continue it, but usually I see how it helps me, so I do it till it becomes a habit, and then I do it every single day.

So little by little I've found some very good exercises to strengthen my body and I've been doing them for many years. The reason I like them so much is that you're lying flat—you don't have to stand or run. Just lie there. And it doesn't take much time to do them all.

I didn't start them for sexual reasons, it just worked out that they've made my body so supple that I can be a contortionist during lovemaking, and that's terrific. I told my husband that I used to work at the circus as an acrobat. He loved the fact that I could twist my legs around him, climb all over his body, move my back in all different directions, lift my legs high in the air, spread them wide, then put them around his thigh with a leg-lock. It's fun to be limber!.

And it's all because of my innocent, simple little daily exercises in bed.

I do them for all the different parts of my body.

First I start with lying flat on my bed, without a pillow, and I do a spine exercise to strengthen my back.

I fold my arms across my chest and first push my lower back down into the mattress, then push my butt down (which raises my tummy), then down again pushing my lower back to the mattress, then butt down. I do that thirty times. Then I hold my lower back down for the count of seven, then my butt down for seven, then the last six times I take turns—I push my lower spine down to the mattress, then my butt down, till fifty.

It so happens that moving your back up and down is great for lovemaking, but I didn't think of that till I got married.

The next exercise is sit ups. I put my hands behind my head with my elbows point-ing forward and do fifty sit ups, which strengthen my tummy muscles, then fifty sit ups which strengthen my back when my elbows are pointing outward to the sides, then the last fifty with my elbows pointing forward which again strengthens my tummy muscles.

So I work both tummy and back muscles.

Strong back muscles will help get rid of back pain because the muscles can now hold your spine in the right position and help you stand up straight. It's pathetic to see a well-dressed, nice looking man or woman who's slumping forward, all bent over. Or even a teener whose shoulders are humped forward. You can imagine what that does to your intestines and all your organs.

My posture improved a lot once I started the sit ups. I was never a slouch, but I sure didn't stand as straight as I do now.

All these moves are also important for lovemaking. Strong back muscles help control your torso, which needs to move a lot when you're in the midst of getting hot and very sexy. You sure don't want back pains to start at that point.

Next I work on my neck. Lying flat on my back, again no pillow, I turn my neck as far to the right as it'll go, hold it for a count of ten, come back straight, now turn my head to the left as far as it'll go, hold it for ten, then go back and forth, right all the way, left all the way, right, left, for a count of thirty.

The last two exercises are for my legs and back. Lying flat, I raise both legs straight up, then bring my knees down toward my chest so I can grasp my toes and feet, then push my legs, with my hands holding them, as hard as I can for a count of ten.

I now let go of my hands and with my legs and feet straight up, I spread my legs as far as I can making a large V, then close them, then go down a bit and spread them again and close them, and keep going down and spreading and closing them till they're still straight out in front of you and you almost reach the bottom on ten, then do the same thing going slowly up to fifteen when you reach the top, then slowly back down to twenty, and up again to the top when you reach twenty five.

Needless to say, getting those spreading-your-legs muscles working is important to a woman in lovemaking.

The last exercise I do is for a strong back. About fifteen years ago I had this terrible pain in my lower back, so bad that when I went on a cruise with my husband he ordered a wheelchair to be at the gangplank for me to enter the ship. And he used it throughout the cruise wheeling me around the deck. It was the worst back pain I've ever had.

When we came back to New York I started going to an acupuncturist twice a week, and very slowly the pain started subsiding, until after about six weeks when it was still somewhat painful, the pain totally disappeared and never came back.

Because I wanted to make sure it never came back, I called a friend in Philly and he gave me the name of his orthopedist who he said could give me some exercises to strengthen my back. He gave me one that's so good I've done it every day since then, and my back muscles are like steel—they really hold up my architectural structure better than any man-made gizmo, including a brace.

You again lie flat, no pillow, body straight, legs straight out in front of you, hands next to body, then you slowly raise—your head and torso, and your arms (still close to your body) and legs—raise them all about ten to twelve inches up. You are now balanced on your upper butt. Then you slowly go down till your body is flat on the mattress again. Do this slowly up and down ten times.

Doing all the exercises takes about ten to fifteen minutes, depending on how slow or fast you do them.

It's not easy at first, but it becomes easier every day you do them. You're using muscles you probably have never used before. It makes your lower back feel very powerful because those muscles are so much stronger than they've ever been.

These in-bed exercises can make a real difference in the way your body feels, and to make sure that lovemaking is not a scenario of pain, but always feeling fabulously exciting and delicious.

As long as two people stay sexually "in love", they will never part.

8
Cheating Will Always Destroy Marriage

Because I know the difference between love and in-love, I know that if a man is a skirt chaser he is absolutely not in love with his wife. He probably still loves her, maybe even a lot, but he's not in love with her.

And the same goes for a woman—if she is a trouser chaser, she only loves her husband, possibly very much, but she is not in love with him.

The most important thing to remember is that you can be in love only with one person.

I don't mean only one person in your lifetime, I mean one person at a time.

And always remember that if a person cheats, that person may love his or her spouse, but is definitely not in love.

If your marriage is at all valuable to you, you must realize this and start to work on heating up your spouse and making sex so great at home that neither one of you would ever think of looking elsewhere for your orgasms.

These are the steps you must do to accomplish this:

1. Make sure both you and your spouse are sexually healthy, that your blood vessels are clear of heavy metals and other gunk, so blood can flow freely to male penis, female mini-penis-clit and nipples—without this, neither will feel super-sexy or be able to orgasm easily. (See CH 3: EDTA)

2. Begin to understand and use loving terms (Honey, Darling Sweetheart,

Baby) with your spouse—and say "I love you" as often as you can—you can't say it too often! The more you love her, the more she'll love you and the more you love him, the more he'll love you. *There is no saturation point with love.*

3. Focus totally on your wife when you are "heating her up"— you want a hot wife, so let her know she's the most important person in your life—don't even consider satisfying yourself till you've driven her wild with passion. You have no idea how your focused pleasure on her body will let her know how much you really love her.

4. And when you wives decide to give your husband oral sex, you must focus on his whole body, touch his butt, his thighs, his stomach, then give all your focus to his penis and lavish it with your lips and tongue, making it wet so your hand can help your tongue

113

stimulate it and give him a "quickie" orgasm.

There's a form of cheating that a few people have tried to legitimatize—open marriage. In fact, a book was written in 1972 titled "OPEN MARRIAGE", by George and Nena O'Neill. Polyamory—literally "multiple loves"—is a word that describes open relationships. It's believed that 4 to 9% of U.S. adults practice polyamory.

George and Nena O'Neill were anthropologists, and I met them years ago when we were on a TV show together, they with "Open Marriage", and I with one of my books. I thought they were totally wrong then and I still do.

One of the tenets in their book states that jealousy is not an inherent part of human nature, and that man is not sexually monogamous by nature, which any thinking, rational person knows is not true.

George O'Neill was known as a ladies' man according to Jeanette Volckmar, a friend of the O'Neills. She states that Nena made an attempt at having lovers other than her husband to equalize the relationship with him, but she believes it was a very painful part of the marriage.

She says that Nena later realized that they had underestimated jealousy when writing the book. And she thereafter spent a lot of her professional life repudiating her association with open marriage and sexual non-exclusivity within a relationship.

According to William Raspberry in "Marriage Thoughts" from *The Capital*, long after their book, Nena O'Neill stated, "Sexual fidelity is not just a vow in a marriage, or a moral or religious belief, but a need associated with our deepest emotions and our question for emotional security. Infidelity is an extremely threatening situation."

Ms. Volckmar says that when Nena later interviewed the subjects of "Open Marriage" she found only a few with sexually open marriages were still married.

Of the one hundred or so couples from the first book, the longest sexually open marriage was two years.

I had a close girlfriend who was a success-ful Hollywood movie writer, and was married

for many years to a businessman. She con-
fided to me that she'd had a very exciting
"romp" with a big movie star who was a
gorgeous guy and a very good actor.

She'd also told her husband about it and
she said he was okay with it because it was
with a famous movie star, which I found dis-
turbing.

One night when I was in L.A. to do a TV
show and she was away on business, she
called me and told me her husband wanted to
take me out for dinner.

We went to a popular place in West L.A.,
and in the middle of the dinner, he told me he
wanted to go to bed with me and would like
to come back to the Beverly Hills Hotel with
me and make love.

I was beyond shocked, and told him I
couldn't believe he would cheat on his wife,
and with her girlfriend at that. But the
biggest shock was when he told me it was his
wife's idea—my girlfriend—for him to do it.

It honestly made me sick, and I never saw
either one of them again.

On WebMD I saw a story titled "The
Truth About Open Marriage", and one fellow

named Chris said that handling the "fear response" in sexual partners can be a problem, and he says that sometimes he has to assure his different partners that his interest in others doesn't mean that his interest in them has lessened.

For those of us who want to always be #1 in our beloved's life, who could even imagine another person being #2 (and trying to become #1)?

Talk about insecurity in a marriage! Why not just stay friends and date whomever you both want?

Chris also states that he has his own envy and jealousy problems when he sometimes feels that his sexual partner is giving more time and energy to another than they are to him. Plus a real problem arises when, again, a "secondary" partner wants to become a primary one.

What a bunch of masochists!

Louanne Cole Weston, PhD, MFT, WebMD's sex and relationship expert and a California marriage and family therapist, believes that a benefit that polyamerists have is that sexual monotony seldom sets in.

I'll bet it doesn't.

But I'll bet a lot of anxiety, worry, insecurity and stress do.

Wouldn't it be more constructive for the partners in a marriage if they work to make their own sex lives more exciting, keeping their sexual love within the intimacy of their marriage rather than having sex with other people, thereby breaking down any intimacy between the married couple?

And one of the side effects of their learning to make the sex between the two of them incredibly exciting is that there's the possibility that they would fall in love again, and this time it could be long-lasting and cheat-proof.

Again I bring up love and in love. If a married couple love each other but are not in love with each other, their marriage days are not cheat-proof. And polyamory will certainly rush the end of their togetherness if they decide to share their bodies with other couples.

However, if two married people are in love and cherish each other and adore each other's bodies, they would no more share the body of their beloved with another man or woman than they would take a gun and kill that body.

As long as two people stay sexually "in love", they will never part.

9
"Forsaking All Others"

After you've fallen in love you both decide you want to get married. You, the woman, love your man so much you want to be his wife and love and take care of him the rest of your life. You, the man, love your woman so much you want to be her husband so you can love and take care of her the rest of your life.

So you go to the county clerk's office, get a marriage license, then go to a priest/minister/rabbi/county clerk and get married. One of these officials has a book (or has it memorized) and recites the following:

"Do you, John, take this woman, Mary, to be your lawfully wedded wife, to have and to hold, from this day forward, in sickness and in health, forsaking all others, till death do you part?"

"I do."

Do you, Mary, take this man, John, to be your lawfully wedded husband, to have and to hold, from this day forward, in sickness and in health, forsaking all others, till death do you part?

"I do."

Whoever wrote the marriage vows was very sensitive to the needs and possible problems of each partner. The vows are beautifully written with strong commitments for the husband and wife to try to ensure a successful marriage.

I believe the most important of all the vows is "forsaking all others". This means only one thing—that your spouse is always first, always numero uno. Your husband is #1 above all others, and your wife is #1 above all others.

Now obviously if one of your kids is sick,

THE SEXUALLY DELICIOUS MARRIAGE

then both of you are going to make that child first until he or she is well again. Or if one of your mothers has an accident, both of you would put her first till she's healed. These are not normal circumstances.

But in day to day life when there are no major problems, it is urgently important that your spouse knows he or she comes before anyone or anything else in your life. That's why it's part of the marriage vows.

I recently saw a WebMD feature by Kate Coyne from a *Good Housekeeping* Magazine interview with Dr. Phil McGraw, star of the big hit TV show, *Dr. Phil*, and his wife of over thirty years, Robin.

Dr. Phil is a clinical psychologist and author of several bestselling books. I've never seen his show, but I have seen him being interviewed on other shows, and I greatly admire his common-sense advice.

Dr. Phil and Robin had many good workable ideas for couples, but the special one that I liked best was when he said: "First of all, I don't believe in divided loyalties. When you're married, your loyalty, first and foremost, is to your spouse . . ."

That's exactly what "Forsaking all others" is about.

Thank you Dr. Phil and Robin!

There are a few well-known married couples who are or have been exceedingly happy in their marriages:

President Ronald Reagan and Nancy Reagan,

Helen Gurley Brown and David Brown,

President George W. Bush and Laura Bush,

Paul Newman and Joanne Woodward,

Betsy and Walter Cronkite,

Janice and Billy Crystal,

Vice President Al Gore and Tipper Gore, etc.

You just know that Ronnie always placed Nancy first in his life and that Nancy adored her husband and always put him #1.

They had two children together, Patty and Ron Jr., plus he had two children from

123

his previous marriage to Jane Wyman, Maureen and Michael. Maureen and Michael appeared to be very well-adjusted and certainly became successful, Maureen working with her father as a political activist for the Republican party and Michael as a very popular talk-show host for Talk America and in San Diego on KSDO-AM.

Patty and Ron, Jr. seemed to be not as close to their parents as their step-siblings and gave out several interviews stating that their mother and father were so wrapped-up in their marriage that they felt "left-out".

Well, their parents chose #1 for each other, which is the way it's supposed to be. From my late husband Gary Stevens, who was an old and good friend of Ronnie's going back to their Warner Brothers days when Gary arranged all Ronnie's many radio and newspaper interviews and accompanied him to all of them, to when Gary put Warners into the TV biz in the mid-50s (and they kept in touch all the years after), Ronnie took great care of all his kids—when they needed him and Nancy, they were there always.

But other than that, Ronnie adored Nancy

and she adored him. And that's why they had such an incredibly happy marriage.

Helen Gurley Brown, beautiful, smart, sexy and very clever, who put Cosmopolitan magazine on the map and made it one of the all-time top mags in the world (she now heads fifty-nine international editions), and her husband David Brown, big-time charmer and movie producer of "Jaws", "The Sting", "A Few Good Men", and a ton of other block-buster films, have been married since 1959.

I know both of them, and what a dynamite couple they are. He is absolutely #1 with Helen, and she's definitely #1 with David, and anybody who's read Cosmo or any of Helen's bestselling books knows that exciting sex has always been a very important part of their marriage.

No matter which political party you belong to, you'll have to admit that President George W. Bush has a great marriage with his wife Laura, and even though he didn't put his wife first when he was a practicing alcoholic, she straightened him out by giving him an ultimatum: It's me or the bottle, and she won.

And ever since then, you just know and feel and see how much they love each other, and that he always puts his wife first. And it's easy to see how she always puts him #1, and that cannot be there if there isn't a deep love and fulfilling and exciting sex life.

Paul Newman and his wife Joanne Woodward have been married for over 50 years, and you can tell by looking at them together that it's a happy marriage. I met Paul many years ago when he visited a Marcel Marceau mime class I was taking in West Los Angeles, and all the females there were excitedly going up to him to talk. He was embarrassed about it, and was obviously only interested in the Marceau mime technique, not salivating females.

Right around that time he made his famous remark about faithfulness that was published in newspapers around the world, "Why fool around with hamburger when you have steak at home?"

I met Walter and Betsy Cronkite several times with my late husband Gary Stevens (who was the producer of Walter's earliest TV show in the 50s), and they were such an adorable couple together—she with her fey sense of humor and Walter laughing at everything she said. You could just tell their marriage was full of love and laughs. And the fact that they touched a lot meant the sexual spark was there.

They were married fifteen days short of sixty-five years. She died on March 15, 2005, and they were married on March 30, 1940.

Comedian Billy Crystal and his wife Janice have been married thirty-eight years and are still very much in love. I watched the TV special about him at "The Kennedy Center Mark Twain Prize For American Humor" in Washington D.C., and when he was onstage and his wife was up in the gallery watching, he spoke lovingly about her and you could see her wipe away her tears. They're emotionally very close and from someone who knows them came the "news" that they have a strong sexual bond.

But I knew it before she told me.

And Vice President Al Gore and his wife Tipper arc very happily married and you know from looking at them that they have a very healthy and exciting sex life. You cannot have that great warmth for each other without the sexual spark in your marriage.

There are many, many more successful marriages all over the world, and to be successful, each one has to have delicious sexual excitement between the partners. If it isn't there, the marriage will probably eventually come to an end. It's as simple as that.

"In love" is delicious sexual excitement.

As long as two people stay sexually "in love", they will never part.

Afterword

The three most precious things in my life are love, humor and music. All three are important to an "in-love" relationship.

The deep love expressed between two people in a sexually delicious marriage is as close to heaven as we'll ever get. And a sense of humor that keeps the two laughing is another super-important factor in a happy marriage.

Last is beautiful music with sensitive, loving lyrics, and my all-time favorite love song, *My One and Only Love*, tells of tender love with total body and soul surrender to one's beloved.

> ". . . the touch of your hand is like heaven, a heaven that I've never known . . .

> . . . in the hush of night while I'm in your arms, I feel your lips so warm and tender . . .

> . . . every kiss you give sets my soul on fire, I give myself in sweet surrender, My one and only love."

Beautiful music by Guy Wood and loving, sensual, "in love" lyrics by Robert "Bobby" Mellin, who was a dear friend with a beautiful soul.

Some other great "in love" songs are: *Night and Day, You Go To My Head, Midnight Sun, How Deep Is The Ocean?* When you and your beloved listen to each song, you'll know exactly what I mean.

As long as two people stay sexually "in love", they will never part.

Suggested Books
to Read

The China Study by T. Colin Campbell is a great book, easy to read, incredibly interesting, and the absolute best book I ever read about how the foods you eat determine your health and the way you feel, from heart problems to cancer, from brain attacks (strokes) to arthritis, etc. This is a must-read for all of you who want to learn about your precious body and how to feel great!

Psycho-Cybernetics, by Maxwell Maltz, M.D., who came up with the term "self-image psychology", and wrote a very interesting

book which helped me years ago to understand myself better than I ever had.

Your Body's Many Cries For Water, by Dr.
Batmanghelidj, M.D., is the book that made
me a water-drinker (and much healthier),
and is very important to read for your own
health and for the health of all those you love.
It explains exactly why your body needs
hydrating, and what happens to your organs
when you don't drink enough water.

Power Through Constructive Thinking, by
Emmett Fox, is a very positive message by a
man who's written many inspirational books.
What makes this super-special is the chapter
called "The Seven Day Mental Diet". I read
this when I was very young and the mental
diet helped me immensely to overcome all
the negative thoughts trying to overwhelm
and undermine me. But I warn you, this mental diet is tougher than any other kind of diet
you've ever tried before!

*The Healing Factor: Vitamin C Against
Disease*, by Irwin Stone, the biochemist

responsible for Linus Pauling's interest in, and study of, Vitamin C. In Stone's book you'll learn that this incredibly curative vitamin is not a vitamin at all, but ascorbic acid, a product of the liver that man lost millions of years ago (and must now add to his diet), that animals still retain. He shows that animals manufacture Vitamin C in their livers—those not under stress make about 3,000 mg. a day, and when under stress, they make over 10,000 mg a day. The USRDA, (Recommended Daily Allowance), is <u>60</u> mg. a day!!!!

Vitamin C and the Common Cold, is by Linus Pauling, the brilliant Nobel Prize winner who was the first to get the world interested in Vitamin C. This book will show you how you can stop all colds and many other sicknesses by taking enough ascorbic acid (he tells you how much) to build up your immune system.

The Prophet, by Kahlil Gibran is a poetic masterpiece in which Gibran speaks of love, marriage, work, giving, joy, sorrow, pain, friendship, pleasure, and death in such beautiful words you will never forget this magnificently written book or its message.

Self-Analysis by Dr. Karen Horney, is one of the best books about how to analyze your own mind, written by one of the world's most well-known psychoanalysts.

The Essays of Ralph Waldo Emerson, by Ralph Waldo Emerson, who was an American essayist, philosopher, and poet. His mind is the most brilliant of any mind I've ever encountered, living or dead. Someone dear to me gave me *The Complete Works of Emerson* when I was nineteen, and the insights I've received from this brilliant writer after re-reading his essays every year, have helped me in every part of my life:

Self Reliance	Compensation
Love	Friendship
Spiritual Laws	Heroism
The Over-Soul	Circles
Intellect	Character

There are many more essays—I just

picked my favorites. Each one of these essays is short but packed with thought-provoking ideas and insights that will stimulate your mind so that you'll be better equipped to problem-solve.

Passages by Gail Sheehy, one of my favorite authors, is an in-depth look at the experiences of others (one hundred fifteen interviews) showing the many internal and external forces acting on us in different stages of our lives. There are passages we take leading us through our 20s, 30s and 40s to what we hope and pray will be our best years in the final decades of our lives.

Kosher Sex, by Rabbi Shmuely Boteach, a brilliant thinker, who wrote this book with constructive ideas for marrieds, and some truly great advice for spouses who are apart for any length of time.

Here are a few good authors who have written some important non-fiction books: Bernard Goldberg, *Bias*, Dick Morris, *Rewriting History*, Bill O'Reilly, *Culture*

Warrior, Sean Hannity, *Deliver Us From Evil,* Michael Savage, *The Savage Nation*, and Laura Ingraham, *Power To The People*.

Times Three by Phyllis McGinley, won the Pulitzer Prize in 1961. She's a brilliant and witty author, and my late aunt. Just recently a CD came out on Amazon (amazon.com), *The Voice Of The Poets: American Wits*, with Ogden Nash, Dorothy Parker, and Phyllis McGinley, with commentary by J.D. McClatchy, editor of *The Yale Review*. This new CD was reviewed by *Audio File*: "I fell in love with Phyllis McGinley. Her best efforts are not just deeply funny but also radically true." So now you can hear these wonderfully witty authors read their own wonderfully witty poetry.

You're welcome, Aunt Phyllis. . . .

Other Books by Naura Hayden

***How to Satisfy a Woman <u>Every</u> Time
. . . and have her beg for more!***
- A marriage manual and a marriage saver!
- The first and <u>only</u> book that tells a man <u>exactly</u> how!
- *The New York Times* bestseller, 62 weeks, #**1**
- *Publishers Weekly* hardcover nonfiction bestseller #**1**
- Published in **Braille**!
- "With this book of revelation, Hayden takes her place as an authority . . . the book carries a giant message." —*The Orlando Sentinel*
- "It really works!" —*Los Angeles Times*
  Hardcover $17.95

How to Satisfy a <u>*Man*</u> *Every Time . . . and have him beg for more!*

- A marriage manual and a marriage saver!
- The first and <u>only</u> book that tells a woman <u>exactly</u> how!
- "A great help" *—Cincinnati Enquirer*

Hardcover $17.95

GO^OD is Alive and Well and Living in Each One of Us

- A revolutionary self-change book
- For physical, mental, emotional and spiritual growth

Hardcover $19.95

Everything You've Always Wanted to Know About ENERGY but were too weak to ask

- About physical, mental and emotional energy
- Over 2 million copy bestseller
- *The New York Times* bestseller
- On every bestseller list in the country

Hardcover $19.95

Isle of View (say it out loud)

- This book full of love-energy will change your life!
- "This upbeat book follows its predecessor onto the bestseller lists"

—*Publishers Weekly*

Hardcover $19.95

Astro-Logical Love

- A *logical* look at astrology*!*
- It's fun, it's easy, and amazingly accurate!
- "This guidebook will let you evaluate your lovers and friends based on their birthdays."

—*PEOPLE* magazine

Hardcover $22.95

On sale at all bookstores

or

1-888-95-NAURA

or

www.naura.com.

Products I Use
Every Day

1. EDTA   Wonder Labs
                              1-800-992-1672

                                    +

                              www.wonderlabs.com

2. Extra Virgin   So. Pacific Trading Co.
   Coconut Oil   1-888-505-4439
        +   +
   Noni Juice   www.nonipacific.com

3. GH3	1-888-384-1835 + www.realgh3.com
4. Natural Calm	1-800-446-7462 + www.naturalcalm.com
5. COQ10	Health food stores
6. Ginkgo Biloba	Health food stores
7. Naura Hayden's **Dynamite Energy Shake**	Health food stores +
Naura Hayden's **Dynamite Vites**	1-888-99-NAURA + www.naura.com
Naura Hayden's **Vitamints**	

Vitamins I Take Every Day

Each of these vitamins and minerals is needed by my body—and yours! I take the Dynamite Energy Shake + the Dynamite Vites every day, and that's why I feel so great. I promise that if you take them, and try to eat well (just cut out sugar and eat lots of fruits and veggies), and try to move your body even minimally (walk as often as you can), you'll start to feel healthier.

VITAMINS & MINERALS	2 TBSP DYNAMITE ENERGY SHAKE	3 TABS 2X DAY DYNAMITE VITES
Vitamin A (Beta Carotene)	0	15000 mg
Vitamin B1	12.5 mg	75 mg
Vitamin B2	12.5 mg	75 mg
Niacin	62.5 mg	125 mg
Niacinamide	62.5 mg	125 mg

VITAMINS & MINERALS	2 TBSP DYNAMITE ENERGY SHAKE	3 TABS 2X DAY DYNAMITE VITES
Calcium	500 mg	1000 mg
Phosphorus	0	100 mg
Iron	12.5 mg	18 mg
Vitamin B6	12.5 mg	75 mg
Folic Acid	200 mcg	400 mcg
Vitamin B12	50 mcg	100 mcg
Iodine	105 mcg	150 mcg
Magnesium	280 mg	400 mg
Zinc	25 mg	15 mg
Copper	1 mg	2 mg
Biotin	150 mcg	300 mcg
Pantothenic Acid	50 mg	150 mg
PABA	50 mg	150 mg
Choline	500 mg	500 mg
Inositol	500 mg	500 mg
Potassium	500 mg	99 mg
Glutamic Acid HCL	0	100 mg
Papain	50 mg	100 mg
Selenium	50 mcg	100 mcg
Ribonucleic Acid (RNA)	50 mg	100 mg
Betaine	50 mg	100 mg
Molybdenum	50 mcg	0
Chromium	50 mcg	100 mcg
Vanadium	50 mcg	0
Manganese	1.5 mg	5 mg
Vitamin C	0	1500 mg
Citrus Flavanoids	0	50 mg
Vitamin D	0	1500 IU
Vitamin E	0	200 IU